The KidHaven Science Library

Lasers

by P. M. Boekhoff and Stuart A. Kallen

KidHaven Press

KidHaven Press, an imprint of Gale Group, Inc.
10911 Technology Place, San Diego, CA 92127

Library of Congress Cataloging-in-Publication Data
Boekhoff, P. M. (Patti Marlene), 1957–
  Lasers / by P. M. Boekhoff and Stuart A. Kallen.
    p. cm. — (KidHaven press science library series)
  Includes bibliographical references and index.
  Summary: Provides a concise overview of lasers, focusing on conception of the idea, initial research, and the overall uses of lasers.
  ISBN 0-7377-0944-8 (hardback: alk. paper)
  1. Lasers—Juvenile literature. [1. Lasers.] I. Kallen, Stuart A., 1955– II. Title. III. Series.
  TA 1682 .B64 2002
  621.36'6—dc21

  2001002184

Contents

Chapter 1
A Bright Idea 4

Chapter 2
Early Laser Research 14

Chapter 3
Lasers in Medicine 23

Chapter 4
Lasers and Technology 31

Glossary 42

For Further Exploration 43

Index 45

Picture Credits 47

About the Authors 48

A Bright Idea

A laser is an invention that makes an intense beam of light that can be used in many ways. Lasers can read and write information on CD players and computers. They are used as very accurate cutting tools in manufacturing and medicine. Laser light shows brighten rock concerts and public celebrations with dancing colors. And lasers are used by the military in many ways, from guiding bombs and airplanes to mapping every part of the earth.

Brighter than the Sun

Long before any of this was possible, Alexander Graham Bell, inventor of the telephone, experimented with the basic scientific ideas used in lasers. In his experiments, Bell tried to harness the energy of the sun. He wanted to use mirrors and sunlight to bounce sound from one place to another. Bell could not make this idea work. The mirrors did not reflect a bright enough beam of light to make his invention, called a photophone,

The military uses lasers for guiding bombs and airplanes.

a reality. But his theory was correct. Today, laser light is used to move sound through high-speed fiber-optic phone lines.

It took the genius of Albert Einstein to invent a way to make a light beam brighter than a sunbeam. Einstein understood that light, heat, and all kinds of energy are given off by tiny **atoms**, which make up all the matter in the universe. In 1905 he announced a new theory about how atoms and light energy are related. Einstein said light is made up of particles called **photons**, that move like waves.

Albert Einstein's ideas about light and energy helped other scientists build lasers.

Atoms, even ones that make up solid objects like a table, are always moving. Einstein understood that atoms sometimes move fast and sometimes move slowly. He believed that energy from light, heat, electricity, or chemical reactions might excite the atoms. This would cause them to move faster and give them extra energy. Once atoms are excited, however, they want to return to their normal state of unexcited movement. When this happens, they give out rays of extra energy in the form of photons or light. Rays of heat or light given off by atoms are called **radiation**.

Emission of Light

In 1917 Einstein said that if excited atoms could be excited or **stimulated** even more, they might give off higher numbers of photons. A beam of light made of many excited photons would be brighter and more powerful than normal light. Einstein called this process stimulated **emission** of light. (When a beam of radiation gives off, or emits, light, it is called emission.)

Because it can produce light that is made more powerful, or **amplified**, stimulated emission can create a powerful laser beam. This super-intense beam was named a laser by combining the first letters of the phrase <u>L</u>ight <u>A</u>mplification by <u>S</u>timulated <u>E</u>mission of <u>R</u>adiation.

Einstein gave scientists the basic understanding they needed to build a laser. But at that time, most scientists were not thinking about how to build a machine to use amplified light energy.

Instead, top scientists were searching for a way to use **microwave** energy. Microwaves are similar to light waves. They both travel at 186,000 miles per second, and both are made up of particles that move in waves. But unlike visible light waves, microwaves are invisible.

Amplified Rays

By the 1940s, scientists were using microwaves in radar to "see" objects far away. During this time, World War II was raging and radar was used to find enemy airplanes.

Radar works by sending out microwave beams. The beams bounce off objects and return to the radar device. There, an image of the object shows up on a screen. By looking at the screen, the radar operator can tell the exact location of an airplane, ship, or other object.

During World War II, enemy scientists learned to block microwave beams so that the image did not bounce back to the screen. American scientists, led by Dr. Charles H. Townes, looked for ways to make more powerful microwave beams that could not be blocked.

After the war, Townes continued his experiments with microwaves. Because microwaves are a lot like light waves, Townes thought they could be stimulated in the same way to become more powerful. He began to experiment with Einstein's

Radar can tell the exact location of an airplane, ship, or other object.

theory, stimulating atoms to produce extra energy in microwaves.

In 1951 Townes had the idea to make a powerful microwave beam using ammonia molecules.

(A molecule is made up of two or more atoms joined together.) Ammonia molecules excite more easily than some others. Townes knew if he could keep the ammonia molecules excited, they might produce a more powerful microwave beam.

The Maser

Townes and two other scientists, Herbert J. Zeiger and James P. Gordon, spent three years on the project. Finally, in 1954, they succeeded. The team had heated ammonia gas, exciting some of the molecules, because heat makes molecules

Charles H. Townes and James P. Gordon invented the atomic clock, called a maser.

move faster and bounce against each other more often. The stimulated molecules then flowed into a chamber called a **resonator**.

Inside the resonator, the excited molecules were further stimulated, bouncing and breaking up and emitting ever-increasing amounts of microwave particles. Soon there were many, many high-energy particles, and the microwaves became very powerful. In less than a second, a powerful ampli-fied microwave beam shot out of a hole in the res-onator. Townes and his team called their invention a maser. (The word *maser* is made up of the first letters of the phrase Microwave Amplification by Stimulated Emission of Radiation.)

The maser, like the laser that followed it, is use-ful for the exact measurement of time and space. The molecules in a maser vibrate at an unchang-ing rate of speed, making the instrument useful as an atomic clock, the most accurate type of clock in the world. The maser also strengthens weak microwave signals given off by distant stars and planets. Astronomers study these signals to find out more about the universe.

The Inventors of the Laser

The maser showed that Einstein's theory could be used to make a practical invention. Townes's next project involved building a working model of his invention to amplify light instead of microwaves.

Theodore H. Maiman looks at the ruby used in the first laser.

In 1957 Townes drew a design for a light machine, which he called an **optical** maser. With the help of his brother-in-law, scientist Arthur Schawlow, he drew detailed plans for his new invention.

Race to Build the Laser

At the same time, several other scientists were also hard at work on similar inventions. These included Nikolai Basov and Aleksandr Prochorov of the Soviet Union and Gordon Gould, a graduate student at Columbia University.

Scientists all over the world were racing to be the first to build a laser, but no one seemed able to make it work properly. Then, in July 1960, Theodore H. Maiman of Hughes Aircraft Company surprised the scientific community and amazed the world when he announced that he had built the first laser. His new invention gave off a thin, bright beam of pure red light. It was called a ruby laser because Maiman passed the light through an artificial ruby to produce the red light.

The invention of the laser is now credited to six people: Townes, Schawlow, Maiman, Basov, Prochorov, and Gould. These men all helped bring Einstein's bright idea to light.

Chapter 2

Early Laser Research

The first laser built by Theodore H. Maiman was small and fairly simple. In the center of Maiman's ruby laser was an artificial rod-shaped ruby about one and one-half inches long. The artificial ruby was the laser's active medium. The active medium contains the atoms or molecules to be stimulated. Maiman stimulated the ruby's atoms with energy from light rays.

Maiman set up a powerful flash lamp so the intensely bright light ran through wires threaded inside a clear glass tube. He heated the glass tube until it softened and could be bent. He then bent the glass tube into the shape of a coil and wound it around the ruby. When he flashed the powerful lamplight through the wires in the coiled glass tube, the photons excited the atoms within the artificial ruby.

The excited atoms were stimulated to give off more photons. Like the ammonia gas chamber in the maser, the ruby acted as a resonator for the excited atoms. But there was no **chamber** for the

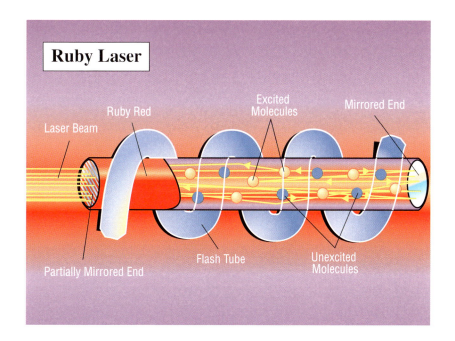

Ruby Laser

Laser Beam

Ruby Red

Excited Molecules

Mirrored End

Partially Mirrored End

Flash Tube

Unexcited Molecules

excited atoms to bounce off of. The structure of the ruby was not solid enough to hold the photons in, so the photons simply passed through it and escaped.

Using Mirrors

Maiman had to find a way to contain and direct the excited atoms. To do so, he painted the round ends of the rod-shaped ruby with silver. The silvered ends became mirrors reflecting the energy back and forth through the rod. The photons bounced back and forth between the mirrors, staying within the ruby rod. With each bounce, the excited atoms picked up more energy and produced more photons.

The newly created photons produced a pure red light. But to direct the light into a beam, the light would have to escape the mirrors and shoot out of the ruby. Maiman made this happen by coating one end of the ruby with only a thin coat of silver, so that it only mirrored back some of the photons, and allowed others to escape.

The photons that escaped shot out of the laser in a thin bright beam of pure red light. Like the maser, the laser was very fast. In only a few millionths of a second, a deep red laser light was created out of the excited photons of the ruby.

Lasers in the Military

After Maiman built the first laser, Hughes Aircraft, the company he worked for, began working on laser weapons for military use. Gordon Gould also began to do research on laser weapons for Technical Research Group, where he now worked.

The U.S. government has poured huge sums of money into laser weapons research, but with few practical returns. In the 1980s, President Ronald Reagan called for a missile shield to defend against nuclear missiles that might be aimed at the United States. In his plan, laser missile detectors mounted on satellites could direct laser-guided missiles to shoot enemy nuclear missiles out of the sky. Experiments with this idea continue, but no such weapons have been developed.

Scientists work on an experimental laser missile shield.

The military has had more success with other forms of laser technology. For example, laser **satellites** are used for secret military communications. Messages are sent in a beam of light that bounces off a satellite. The beam is then reflected to a receiver on earth. Each laser is tuned to one special color, or band, of light, and can only be detected by a receiver tuned to that color. In use, a soldier can receive a message encoded in a beam of light, shot around the earth in a fraction of a second.

Laser Range Finders

The most practical invention of military laser research is the range finder. Laser range finders

Laser range finders can light up targets and aim and guide missiles to the target.

can light up military targets for bombing. They can also aim and guide missiles, carrying a sensor that follows a laser beam to the target.

Lasers, like masers, measure time and space very accurately. The range finder uses lasers to measure the distance, or range, to a military target. It does this by measuring the time it takes for the laser light to travel to the target, and back. Knowing the exact distance to the target helps the soldier hit it.

Another use for laser range finders is to find objects such as trees or mountains in front of low-flying airplanes. The range finder instantly measures the distance between the airplane and objects in its path. Using a laser range finder, planes can be guided very accurately and safely to fly between and over objects that are very close. This allows laser-guided, low-flying military airplanes to avoid detection by the enemy.

Measuring Time and Space

Laser range finders have nonmilitary uses, too. They can be used like giant rulers to measure the distance between houses, roads, and mountains. Surveyors use range finders to create exact and reliable maps. Using lasers placed in satellites orbiting the earth, map makers have measured and charted the entire surface of the earth.

Lasers help scientists see how our planet changes over time. Tiny movements in the earth's

Lasers help scientists understand earthquakes by measuring tiny movements in the earth's crust.

crust are measured by lasers, helping scientists understand earthquakes. Satellite laser range finders help scientists monitor air pollution and changes in the earth's atmosphere that may be related to global warming and other environmental problems. Lasers also gauge wind speed during storms and are used to measure the exact height of clouds at airports.

Lasers are so accurate, they can measure tiny movements over long periods of time and vast distances in space. In 1969 astronauts left mirrors on the moon for measuring the distance from the earth to the moon with a laser beam. Each year, scientists measure the length of time it takes for a laser beam to reach the moon mirror and come back to Earth. In this experiment, scientists found that the moon is moving away from the earth about one and one-half inches a year.

Like a ruler, the laser can be used for making straight lines as well as for measuring. Because laser beams stay in a straight line over very long distances, engineers use them to stay on a straight course while building bridges, digging tunnels, or laying out roads. Laser beams are also used in construction to line up the parts of big structures, such as skyscrapers and ships.

Mirrors placed on the moon help lasers measure the distance between the moon and the earth.

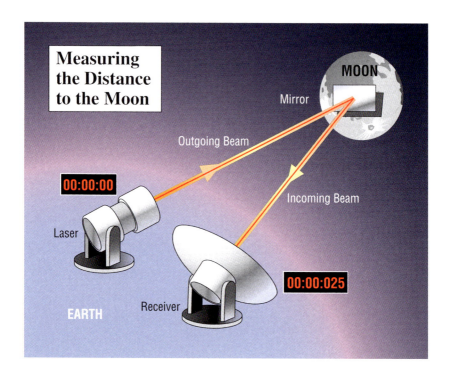

The laser has come a long way since that first bright beam of light shot through Theodore Maiman's ruby laser. Today, the laser is one of the most useful tools of science and industry. It promises to grow in importance in the future.

Chapter 3

Lasers in Medicine

Few tools of the modern age can do as many different jobs as lasers can today. Lasers have hundreds of different uses. They are important tools for the heavy work done in construction and industry. In building construction, lasers drill holes in granite and concrete. In highway construction, they blast tunnels through rock. Lasers can also be found in factories, where they cut and weld large parts for cars, airplanes, and ships.

Lasers have shown their value in fields that require great care and exact, tiny movements. One of these fields is medicine. Today, doctors use lasers for simple jobs such as removing scars, birthmarks, or even tooth decay. Other lasers perform more complex, delicate work such as eye surgery. Laser microtools are lighting up a whole new world of tiny objects for scientists to study and manipulate, such as microscopic DNA molecules and atoms.

Lasers have several advantages over other cutting tools. They never get dull. They never wear

Lasers easily cut holes in concrete and tunnel through rock.

out or break. Because they use a beam of light, they never have to be sharpened or replaced. And lasers work fast—a beam of laser light can cut through thick metal or delicate skin in a few millionths of a second.

No tool can measure and cut more accurately than a laser. Lasers can measure the space between molecules or the space between the earth and the moon, and repeat those measurements exactly, over and over.

Laser Surgery

Since they are the sharpest, most exact cutting tools ever made, lasers are miracle tools in the hands of skilled surgeons. They allow surgeons to make precise cuts in human tissue with more accuracy than a knife called a scalpel. When a doctor cuts a patient during surgery, a steady hand is necessary to make the cut the right depth. Lasers can be adjusted to cut to any depth, so the surgeon can make the cut in just the right place, without worrying about how deep it is.

Besides being more accurate than scalpels, lasers are much cleaner tools. Unlike the scalpel, laser light never gets dirty and never carries

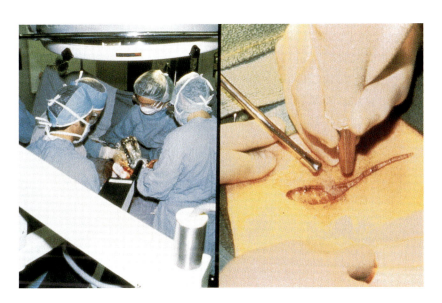

Surgeons are able to make precise, clean cuts in human tissue using lasers.

germs that can be passed to the patient. Scalpels, on the other hand, require very careful cleaning and handling to keep them sterile.

The heat produced by lasers sterilizes and seals the cut as the surgeon makes it. The patient heals faster because the laser heat seals blood vessels so there is less bleeding, swelling, or scarring. And surgery takes less time because the laser can cut tissue in a quick burst of light.

Laser Eye Surgery

One of the most popular uses of laser surgery is to correct vision. The laser beam can be focused to make very thin cuts and welds on the human eye. No other tool could make such clean, thin cuts.

Lasers can correct the sight of people who are nearsighted (can focus only on close objects), far-

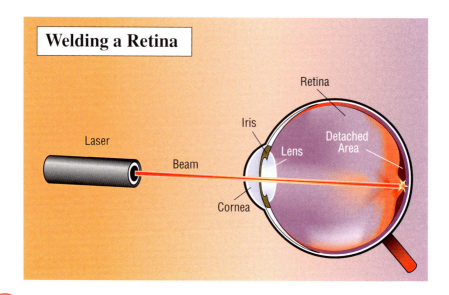

Welding a Retina

Retina

Iris

Detached Area

Laser

Lens

Beam

Cornea

sighted (can see things in the distance), and astigmatic (the eye is curved in a way that distorts distances). These errors in vision are caused when the shape of the cornea, the outer portion of the eye, focuses light rays incorrectly on the retina, the light-sensitive membrane lining the inner eyeball. With laser eye surgery, the laser is used to change the curve of the cornea, making it flatter or steeper, depending on the problem experienced by the patient.

The Surgery Process

First, the laser peels away the cornea, leaving one side attached like a hinge. The doctor then uses a laser to cut and weld the surface underneath the cornea to reshape the curve. The flap is then replaced, and the cornea falls along the new curve. This changes the focus of the eye, so that the image lands correctly on the retina.

The whole operation can take less than fifteen minutes for both eyes, and the patient can be awake during surgery. The eyes are numbed during the procedure, and eyesight leaves for a minute, but sight returns quickly. The operation is painless because each burst of laser light lasts only a small fraction of a second, and the nerves in the eye do not have enough time to signal pain. In most cases, laser eye surgery can be done without long healing time and large costs.

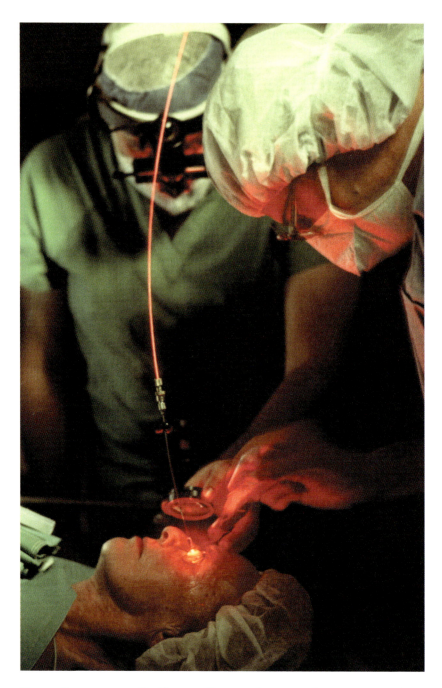

Laser beams can be focused to make very thin cuts and welds on the human eye.

Lasers

Laser Microtools

The newest kind of laser surgery is microsurgery, performed with laser microtools. These tools allow scientists to work with the tiny particles that make up living tissue.

To perform laser microsurgery, laser light is focused through a microscope. Scientists can then see and work with living tissue. They do this by focusing the laser beam on the tissue. The beam traps cells in the tissue. Scientists can then work with the cells by moving the laser beam.

Laser traps use a long low-level laser beam to hold cells in place. Cold temperatures slow down the moving parts within the cell. This allows scientists to remove or add living material without damaging the cell. Laser traps can be used for many tasks, such as fusing two cells together to make a mix of two different species.

While holding material in a laser trap, laser scalpels are used to cut through cell walls to pull out the genetic material known as DNA. The DNA may then be used to transfer genes from one species to another. This technology has been used for such things as changing the DNA of food plants to make them poisonous to insects that eat them.

Scientists are also using laser microtools to study how cells divide and communicate. This research may lead to a better understanding of cancer and birth defects.

Lasers have made surgery a much more exact science. Working with lasers, scientists are able to perform surgery on the most delicate parts of the human body. Even the tiniest parts that make up the living body can be altered by tiny surgical laser tools. In this way, lasers are helping scientists to understand the basis of all life on Earth.

Lasers and Technology

The laser has changed modern life in many ways. In the past several decades, lasers have become part of everyday life in countries across the globe. People depend on them to surf the Internet, send and receive messages, conduct business, and even listen to music.

New ways of using lasers will bring more changes in the future. Scientists are working on a new type of computer, for example, that will run on laser light instead of electricity. Such a computer could carry one thousand times more information than today's machines and would be faster and quieter. With such a computer, lasers could beam a moving, talking image of a person into a room thousands of miles away.

Lasers also offer promise in areas of energy and transportation. For example, lasers are being used to build fuel cells, which store and give off energy. Combined with solar and wind energy sources, fuel cells might someday run nearly every machine on Earth with no pollution.

Lasers and Computers

Lasers are used in a wide array of computerized devices such as scanners, printers, and fax machines. When joined to computers, lasers can read and write. Laser scanners read pages of information thousands of times faster than a person can type them into a computer. Laser printers print clean, clear copy on paper, turning out hundreds of pages per minute.

Laser facsimile systems, or fax machines, send photos and words through telephone lines. The laser beam in the fax machine scans the images, which are then converted into digital signals and sent as electrical energy to another fax machine. There, the energy is changed back to light images, which the laser burns onto a light-sensitive metal drum, which transfers the images to paper.

Laser-Powered Fiber Optics

Faxes and other types of electronic information are transferred through telephone lines by fiber-optic cables that depend on lasers. The cable is made up of hundreds of strands of bendable glass thinner than a human hair yet stronger than steel. One fiber-optic cable can carry vast amounts of information sent through it by a laser beam.

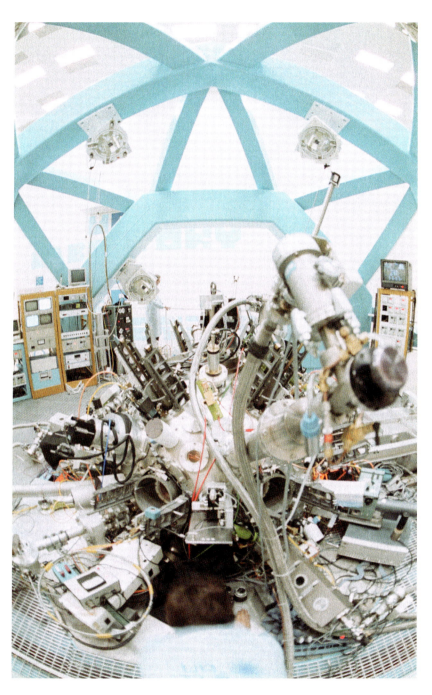

Lasers are used to build fuel cells, which might someday run machines without polluting the environment.

In the early 1990s, laser fiber-optic cables were installed across the United States and many other countries. They were also laid on the bottoms of the Atlantic and Pacific oceans. Laser-powered fiber-optic cables make telephone conversations between countries much clearer. They also make it possible for tens of millions of users to send information around the globe within a matter of seconds over the Internet.

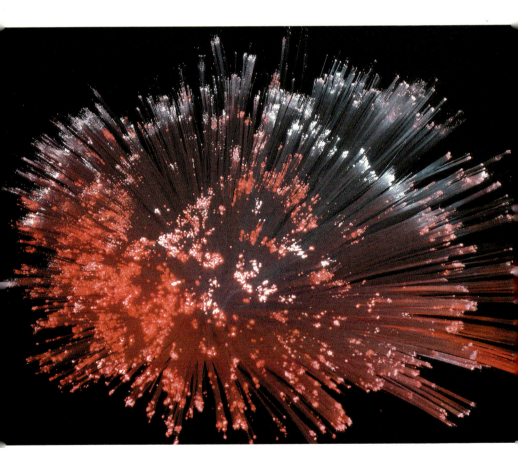

Fiber-optic cables are made up of hundreds of strands of strong, bendable glass.

Laser fiber-optic cables were laid on the bottom of the Atlantic and Pacific oceans.

Holography

Other laser-computer advances allow people to see a photograph as if it were a three-dimensional (or 3-D) image in a room. These images are called **holograms**. When a person looks at a hologram from different angles, it looks real from the front, back, and sides. But if the person reaches out to touch the hologram, his or her hand passes right through as if it were a ghost.

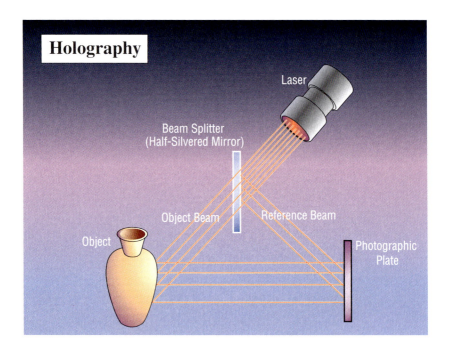

Holography

Laser

Beam Splitter
(Half-Silvered Mirror)

Object Beam

Reference Beam

Object

Photographic
Plate

Holograms are made by shining a laser beam on an object to be photographed. Before the laser beam strikes the object, it is split by a half-silvered mirror, or beam splitter. One of the beams goes from the mirror to a piece of photographic film. The other beam passes through the mirror, bounces off the object, then strikes the film. The two images look like a jumbled gray fog on the film. But when another laser beam is shone through the developed film, a three-dimensional image appears in the beam of light.

Holograms have many uses. They are imprinted into identification cards, such as a driver's license or credit card. Holograms are difficult to make, so it is harder for thieves to make fake cards.

Hologram technology is also applied to the study of microscopic organisms, whose 3-D images can be projected into a room. This allows several scientists to easily study the image without looking into a microscope.

In the future, scientists predict that holographic motion picture cameras will be used to make 3-D movies and television shows that will appear as if they were really taking place in the room of the viewer.

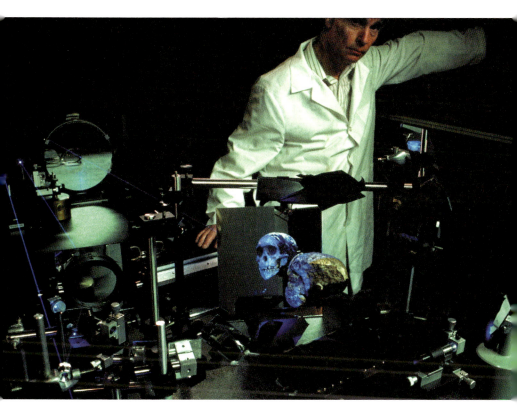

A scientist uses laser technology to create a hologram of a skull.

Laser Fuel Cells

Scientists are also using laser tools to help create a clean energy source called fuel cells that makes power from electricity and water. Fuel cells were invented by Sir William Grove in 1839, and were developed by the National Aeronautics and Space Administration (NASA) in the 1960s to provide electricity and water for astronauts in space. Although they worked well, they were too heavy for practical use and very expensive to produce until laser technology became available.

Laser technology makes pollution-free cars a reality.

Modern fuel cells use ultrathin layers of metal that can be cut only by a high-powered laser. This technology is so important that in 2000, eight of the ten largest companies in the world were interested in the new fuel cells created with lasers. These companies are experimenting with fuel cells to provide energy for transportation, homes, businesses, and electric power plants.

Laser technology has made it possible and practical to drive a pollution-free car. In the year 2000, the first laser-built fuel cell vehicles were put on the road. They are fast and quiet, and they run on hydrogen found in water instead of gas. And they produce drinkable water from their tailpipes instead of pollution. New filling stations using solar cell and wind turbine energy collectors will create the electrical energy to convert the water to hydrogen to fuel the cars.

Lasers of the Future

Laser technology, when combined with other technology, holds many possibilities for changing the world. Laser tools have created the possibility of completely pollution-free energy in our future. New laser technology will allow people to create even thinner, smaller, and lighter fuel cells that will be used to power everything from motorcycles to portable electronic devices.

NASA experiments with laser satellites in hopes that one day travel to distant planets on a beam of light will be possible.

The development of lasers since the 1950s has benefited humankind in hundreds of ways. In the not-so-distant future, people may be riding to distant planets on a beam of light, just as Albert Einstein imagined in the early twentieth century. What scientists may learn from trying to ride a beam of light may be applied to technology on Earth. The laser has been a great tool for making giant leaps in science. The things it may be used for in the future are but a dream of scientists today.

Glossary

amplify: to make larger or more powerful

atom: the smallest basic structure of which all things are made

chamber: an enclosed space

emission: giving off or sending out matter or energy

hologram: a three-dimensional image made with lasers

microwave: a radio wave that produces heat but no visible light

optical: relating to sight, visible light, and light-sensitive devices

photon: an energy particle with no mass or electrical charge

radiation: emission of energy in the form of rays, waves, or particles

resonator: a hollow chamber that permits electric or light waves to vibrate rapidly under controlled conditions

satellite: an object launched into orbit around the earth

stimulate: to excite to activity or increased action

For Further Exploration

N. S. Barrett, *Lasers and Holograms*. New York: Franklin Watts, 1985. Explains how holograms work and describes some of the uses of holograms and lasers.

Mary Virginia Fox, *Lasers*. Inventors & Inventions series. Tarrytown, NY: Benchmark Books, 1995. Information about lasers, the people who invented them, and "amazing facts" about their use.

Nina Morgan, *Lasers*. Austin, TX: Raintree/Steck Vaughn, 1997. A simple, easy-to-understand book about lasers written for a young audience.

Don Nardo, *Lasers: Humanity's Magic Light*. San Diego: Lucent Books, 1990. For advanced readers. Discusses the history of lasers and their uses in such fields as medicine, entertainment, and the military.

Steve Parker, *Lasers: Now and into the Future*. Parsippany, NJ: Dillon Press, 1998. Explains how lasers work, describes ways in which they have revolutionized our lives, and predicts how they may be used in the future.

Matthew Weschler, "How Lasers Work," Howstuff-works website, 2001, www.howstuffworks.com/laser.htm. The first of several pages of information about how lasers work.

Kathryn Whyman, *Rainbows to Lasers.* New York: Gloucester Press, 1989. Introduces the subject of light and includes hands-on science projects.

Index

ammonia, 9–10
atoms, 5–6

Basov, Nikolai, 12–13
beam splitters, 36
Bell, Alexander Graham,
      4–5

cars, 39
computers, 31, 32, 34
construction, 21, 23

DNA, 29

earthquakes, 19–20
Einstein, Albert, 5–7
energy sources, 31–32,
      38–39
engineers, 21
eye surgery, 26–27

facsimile machines, 32
fiber optics, 32, 34
fuel cells, 31–32, 38–39

genetics, 29
Gordon, James P., 10
Gould, Gordon, 13, 16
Grove, Sir William, 38

holography, 35–37
Hughes Aircraft
      Company, 13, 16

Internet, the, 34

lasers (Light
      Amplification by
      Stimulation Emission
      of Radiation), 6
      advantages of, 23–24,
            25–26
      invention of, 11–13
      military use of, 16,
            18–19
light, 5, 6

Maiman, Theodore H.,
      13–16
masers, 8–11
medicine, 23, 25–27,
      29–30
microscopes, 29
microsurgery, 29–30
microwaves, 8–10
military, 16, 18–19
mirrors, 15–16
missile shields, 16
molecules, 9–10

name, meaning of, 6
National Aeronautics and
 Space Administration
 (NASA), 38

optical masers, 12

photons, 5, 14–16
photophones, 4–5
pollution, 20
Prochorov, Aleksandr,
 12–13

radar, 8
radiation, 6
range finders, 18–19
Reagan, Ronald, 16
research, 29
resonators, 10
ruby lasers, 13, 14–16

satellites, 16, 18, 19, 20
Schawlow, Arthur, 12, 13
space exploration, 21, 38
surgery, 25–27, 29–30
surveyors, 19

Technical Research
 Group, 16

telephone lines,
 32, 34
three-dimensional (3-D)
 images, 35–37
Townes, Charles H.
 lasers and, 11–13
 masers and, 8–10
traps, 29

uses, 4
 construction and, 21,
  23
 earthquakes and,
  19–20
 engineers and, 21
 medicine and, 23,
  25–27, 29–30
 military and, 16,
  18–19
 pollution and, 20
 space exploration and,
  21, 38
 surveyors and, 19
 weather and, 20

weather, 20
World War II, 8

Zeiger, Herbert J., 10

Picture Credits

Cover Photo: © Hank Morgan/VHSID Lab/ECE
   Department, University of Massachusetts/
   Science Source/Photo Researchers
© Bettmann/CORBIS, 7, 11, 12, 21
© Jonathan Blair/CORBIS, 37
© CORBIS, 35
Chris Jouan, 15, 22, 26, 36
© The Military Picture Library/CORBIS, 18
© Charles O'Rear/CORBIS, 28
© Roger Ressmeyer/CORBIS, 17, 20, 33, 34
© Reuters NewMedia Inc./CORBIS, 5, 38, 40
© Telegraph Colour Library/FPG, 9, 24
Unlimited Solution Audio Visual Inc., 25

P. M. Boekhoff has cocreated ten children's books on the subjects of art, ecology, and Native Americans, and illustrated many book covers. In addition, Ms. Boekhoff creates theatrical scenics and other large paintings. In her spare time, she writes poetry and fiction, studies herbal medicine, and tends her garden.

Stuart A. Kallen is the author of more than 150 nonfiction books for children and young adults. He has written extensively about Native Americans and American history. In addition, Mr. Kallen has written award-winning children's videos and television scripts. In his spare time, Mr. Kallen is a singer/songwriter/guitarist in San Diego, California.